A Single Mom Talks to God

Karen O'Donnell Taylor

Liguori
ONE LIGUORI DRIVE
LIGUORI MO 63057-9999

Imprimi Potest:
Richard Thibodeau, C.Ss.R.
Provincial, Denver Province
The Redemptorists

ISBN 0-7648-1139-8
Library of Congress Catalog Card Number: 2003113215
© 2004, Karen O'Donnell Taylor
Printed in the United States of America
04 05 06 07 08   5 4 3 2 1

To order, call 1-800-325-9521
www.liguori.org
www.catholicbooksonline.com

Contents

In Loving Memory of Diane T. Rund
A Woman of Strength

Introduction

Becoming a mother was one of my greatest blessings, and I treasure my children above all else! But becoming a single mom was never in my plans. Who would ever choose to walk this difficult path of parenthood alone?

Unfortunately many women must face this task. This book is the result of my own life as a single mom, a life in which my prayer very often takes the form of talks with God. The prayers I offer here were written as if God were speaking through me.

I consider them a gift. For as difficult a road as this is, my faith in God is the one constant in my life—the one reason I continue to make it through those days when I'd just like someone else to be responsible for a change.

I recently published a book entitled *Praying Through Your Divorce,* written for anyone faced with that difficult path. But this book is expressly for women— women like you who are challenged every day as women who are not single moms are never challenged.

No one but a single mom can ever really know what it's like to raise a child alone. It is lonely, frustrating, and exhausting. Yet, too, it can be rewarding, love-engendering, and fulfilling.

I admire every woman who, through whatever circumstances, is a single mother. You deserve the respect of everyone, for you are doing alone a job that two people together often find difficult and extremely challenging!

One Mother's Day, I was attending Mass at a small, comfortable parish. The priest there had all moms stand up for a round of applause. He specifically mentioned single mothers and what a tough job they had. I remember feeling so proud—and so should you!

As my children go through the teenage years just now, I feel doubly challenged. There are some days I don't think I'll make it through! But somehow, with God's help and the support of many friends, I do make it.

In that spirit, I offer many thanks to my children, Ryan and Meghan, my greatest gifts. I love you bigger than the sky! Thanks also to my family and wonderful friends for their constant support and to Sue, my editor, for her help and belief in this book.

I hope that these prayers, these talks with God, help you a little bit on your challenging journey. I hope you smile knowingly at some and feel validated by others. Above all, take comfort in the fact that you are not alone!

I wish a bounty of blessings for you and your children, a home that is a garden of peace and serenity, and a joyous life of new beginnings!

Karen

About Myself

Overwhelmed

Help! I'm overwhelmed today, Lord. (I feel like that nearly every day lately.) There are so many tasks to handle and only *one* of me.

Please help me to quiet my thoughts and simply do my best. Let me realize that my *best* is more than good enough for you. It is all you ask, and it should be all I ask of myself.

Help me break down big tasks into small ones. Let me learn a crucial lesson in this life of single motherhood—how to say "no."

Such a short, simple little word. Teach me to say "no" more to others' unreasonable demands and "yes" more to myself!

Energy

Too bad you didn't make an energy pill that all of us single moms could take. (What a success that product would be!)

We single moms seem to constantly lack three things—time, money, and energy!

Could it be that this energy thing is most in my control? I think so.

First let me learn not to squander my energy, not to waste it on unimportant things. Let me save it for the more difficult tasks I must do.

Let me learn to take breaks and pamper myself once in a while so I can come back renewed and recharged.

Give me all the energy I need for my job, my home, and most especially my children. Give me the energy, no matter how tired I am, to do the very best job I possibly can.

My faith gives me energy as does my love for my children.

Time

There's so little time, Lord, to accomplish all the things I must do. I know there are only so many minutes in the day. But can you please show me how to make peace with these limits?

It seems that at the end of every day, there is still a stack of unfinished tasks. Each day the list gets bigger because I cannot finish them all.

Please help me to make better use of my time. Perhaps I can make to-do lists that give priority to things that I must do today and identify other things I can let go for a day or two. Maybe I can delegate some chores for my children to do.

I also need to learn to say "no," with grace and dignity. Learning to say "no" will give me more time to say "yes" to all the things I must do!

Let my times be rich and full, and let there be a bit of leisure time in my life for renewal and recharging.

Freedom

Let me enjoy this new freedom, Lord. I may not have all the time I used to, but I certainly have more choices.

I decide now what meals to make, what movies to watch, and where the money goes.

It is a scary and yet heady feeling to be completely in charge.

Let me celebrate my freedom today! Let me enjoy the myriad of choices in my life, and help me to always make the *right* decisions.

For My Future

I pray today, God, for my future. Sometimes it scares me to think about it. I'm so afraid of spending the rest of my life alone. I always thought I'd be part of a married couple.

Let me look at the future not with fear but with anticipation.

I am a talented, capable woman. There are so many delightful possibilities! I can accomplish much, as long as I have a positive attitude.

Let me not worry so much about the future, about what or whom it will bring. Let me concentrate instead on the *present* and make my days the fullest and richest they can possibly be.

And let me remember my children. I am so lucky to have them. And they ensure that I will never really be *alone*.

Annulment

Though *annul* means *erase,* let me think of it in positive terms, Lord. I will picture this as a new slate. My previous story has been erased, and I am free to write a new one. I can make this a vibrant, joyful life—a fulfilling one for my family and me.

I can color this new life with hope, determination, and beauty. I am the artist of this new canvas, just as you are the divine Creator. Let me draw strength and inspiration from you!

A Hot Bath

Things can get to be too much for me, Lord. When they do, I can retreat and take a hot bath. I can light candles and play soft music. I can have sparkling water, tea, or a glass of wine.

Help me to realize that it's OK to pamper myself. I am a wonderful creation of yours! It is right that I care for myself as well as I care for my own children.

Thank you for this time just for me.

Sleeping Alone

It seems strange sometimes to be sleeping alone, God. I was part of a couple for so long. There were arms to hug me and feet to warm mine. The bed seemed cozy, but now it feels too big for just me!

Please bless my dreams as I sleep alone. Let me find comfort in my bed and be grateful for the time of peace I spend here.

Let me be grateful for that comfort and find release from my troubles as I dream.

Let my dreams be joyous ones—perhaps of a new love that may enter my life soon and maybe warm both my bed and my life.

Stress

Oh, boy, Lord. I may need more than one prayer on stress. I feel like it's been my middle name for years now. When will it let up?

There are so many areas of stress in my life! And there is no one to share the burden with.

If I feel I need to get away from the kids for a little while, there's no one to call out to: "I'll be back later, honey. You handle the kids for now!" The stresses of work and children and finances and every other stress, I bear alone.

Let me remember that I am never completely alone, Lord. I have you to pray to and believe in! How lucky I am to have this faith of mine!

When I am feeling stressed, let me find ways to handle it. Perhaps I can take a cup of tea out on the back steps for a little breather. Maybe I can putter in the garden or the kitchen—bake some brownies to fill our home with sweet smells. Maybe I can take a long walk and just get a fresh perspective for a little while. I can call a friend and hear a reassuring voice say that everything will be all right.

And everything *will* be all right if I believe it will be. And I *do* believe it!

Fresh Flowers

There is no one to buy me flowers anymore, Lord, so I've decided to buy them for myself!

Let me realize that I deserve a little TLC, and I may need to give it to *myself* just now.

I can budget them into my grocery money and skip a few bags of chips or bottles of soda.

I buy one bouquet and split it—some for my kitchen, a single flower for our bathroom, and a few flowers for my desk at work. And when someone at work asks me "Who sent the flowers?" I smile and say, "I did!"

Fresh flowers make me feel wonderful. Each time I look at them, I feel special and loved— and I *am*!

In Sickness

Please be with me while I'm sick, Lord. I don't like being out of commission like this. My kids just want me to snap out of it so I can get back to tending to *their* needs. It's hard for them to see me sick like this.

Help me to tend to my *own* needs for now until I'm better. Help me to relax and take care of myself—not to feel guilty for being sick.

Help me to realize that being sick is out of my control, but taking good care of myself is *within* my control. Let me pamper myself as best I can, get plenty of rest, and *ask* for help if I need it.

Be with me while I'm sick—and when I'm well again, let me be grateful for my health!

Touch

I miss being touched, God, being hugged and caressed. As human beings we crave the sense of touch. I miss this in my life.

But let me find ways to fill this void in my life right now. I can hug my children and my friends more. (Perhaps they crave a hug as much as I do!) I can stroke the soft fur of my pet. Maybe I can even pamper myself by budgeting in an occasional massage!

Let me realize, too, that perhaps one day soon I will find a sweet man to fill my heart with joy—and my arms with warmth!

Keep Me Safe

Keep me safe and healthy, God. I can't even imagine my childrens' lives without me to care for them. As difficult as our lives have been, I know deep down they appreciate all I've done.

So I ask you to help me raise these children of mine until they are strong and can stand on their own. Keep me healthy emotionally, mentally, and physically at least until then, Lord.

Music

Music seems to fill up all the little empty spaces in my life, Lord.

I am grateful for the peace it brings me in quiet times and the energy it gives me as I clean or exercise or chauffeur the kids around.

Thank you for this gift that enhances all the moments in my life, for the melodies and words that touch my heart.

Sleep

This is a prayer for sleep, Lord. It does not come easily for me some nights.

I have so much on my mind, so many worries. At night they dance in my mind, keeping me awake.

Please help me to quiet my mind. Ease my mental burdens so I can sleep. Let me find peace at night so that I can wake up in the morning renewed and ready to face the day.

Hope

I am so grateful for the gift of hope, Lord. Hope is the fuel that keeps me going. It gives me energy even on the darkest days.

Hope helps me to truly believe that things *will* get better. In fact they already have. There is a little more peace in our lives now. And there is so much possibility!

Hope gives wing to possibility, and it carries me more joyfully toward the future!

Gratitude

I pray for more gratitude in my life, Lord. It is so easy to get caught up in all the things we *don't* have. Let me concentrate instead on everything we *do* have.

We have each other. We have a place to rest our heads at night and food on the table. I have work that enables me to provide for my children.

And I have small, sweet joys each day to be thankful for...the smile or hug of my child, a chat with a close friend, a quiet cup of tea, and hope—always hope for a better tomorrow.

Faith

Today I give deep thanks for the gift of faith. How do people cope without faith in you, God?

My life has been difficult. I know I couldn't have made it so far without this awesome gift. My faith gives me an inner strength that carries me buoyantly toward the future.

With faith in my heart, I travel this lonely path with confidence, content in the knowledge that everything *will* indeed be all right.

My children and I are in your loving hands. What better place is there to be than that?

Work in Progress

I've always believed that I'll be a lifelong learner, God. Well, that includes learning about me.

I am a glorious work in progress. I am never done, never finished. There is always something to work on—something I can improve about myself.

I am my own sweet adventure! Each day I discover new things, new strengths or talents I have. I discover new joys and favorites. Sometimes I face new weaknesses or fears as well.

Isn't it wonderful that I'm not perfect?

I am like a sculpture to be molded and refined each day, a unique work in progress!

Together

I pray for two kinds of *together*, Lord.

I pray first for the strength to keep it all to-gether. Keeping my sanity these days is no small task. I could use your help with that! So I ask for your help and blessings with this.

Second, I pray with gratitude that you en-able my little family to stay *together* and not be separated from each other. As I draw strength from you, so we draw strength from each other.

A New Day

Yesterday wasn't so good, Lord. I had a lot of trouble getting through it.

But today is a fresh new page to write on, a new chapter in life's book.

Let me treat yesterday as a crumpled, tossed-out paper—gone and forgotten.

Let me welcome this new day with energy, enthusiasm, and most especially hope.

Love

Am I ever going to find love again, Lord? I am so lonely. Though my life is busy and full, I still feel like something is missing in my life.

I pray that I do find love again—a person who will enhance and enrich my life in abundant ways, a man I will love long and love well as he will love me.

I know he is out there, Lord. Until we meet each other, please bless him and all he may be going through.

Let us find each other soon and love each other completely.

Let the light of love fill my days once again.

Confidence

I don't feel pretty enough or thin enough, and I *know* I'm not so young anymore. I need *confidence*!

There are so many women out there looking for the same thing I am—their soul mate. There's a lot of competition, Lord!

Help me to realize that it's not just the *outside* packaging that's important. It's the *gift inside* that counts.

Let me realize that when I finally give the gift of me, it will be to a man who will treasure me for who I truly am.

But in the meantime as I search for him, please grant me the gift of confidence.

What's for Dinner?

God, how I would love to walk into my house at night, smile, sniff the fragrant air, and say, "Mmm….What's for dinner?"

Unfortunately that scene exists only in my dreams. I'm not the one who *asks* the question but the one who *answers* it.

Give me the energy I need after working all day to walk in the door with a smile instead of a sigh. Let me create a nutritious meal for my family. Let me be grateful for having the means to provide these meals for my family.

A Wife

I know it sounds silly, Lord, but I'm wishing for a wife today! I'm longing for a past me in my present life.

I'm so tired of doing everything myself. If only there were someone to cook the meals, run the errands, care for the children, and complete each task on my never-ending list.

Help me to realize that even though I have all these tasks to do myself, I also have the freedom that goes with being on my own. I am grateful for that.

Let me go easy on myself. My house doesn't have to be perfect and my children won't die from boring meals. Let me realize that I don't need a wife after all—I've got *me*!

Breakfast in Bed

I long for someone to bring me breakfast in bed. I know I deserve it, Lord.

Since there's no one here to wait on me, let me treat myself instead!

Let me create a simple breakfast for myself and enjoy it in my cozy bed. I feel special when I take the time to pamper myself. Breakfast in bed not only nourishes my body but my spirit as well!

Recharge My Batteries

I need my batteries recharged, Lord! I feel sapped of my energy.

Please zap me with more energy! Give me the physical, emotional, and spiritual fuel I need for all my daily tasks and trials.

Recharge my batteries, Lord!

Mother's Day

I feel too tired to enjoy Mother's Day, Lord. There's no husband to ensure that today is special for me. And I don't feel like going to the effort myself.

Let me make this effort anyway! Let me take my family out to eat. Let us celebrate the mother I am. I may not be the perfect mother, but I give myself an A+ for effort.

Let me be grateful this day for the gift of motherhood. Becoming a mother was the single greatest gift of my life. Let me relish that gift today.

Romance

There is no romance in my life, Lord, except for romance novels and tearjerker movies. These are poor substitutes for the real thing.

I wonder if there'll ever be romance again in my life. I'm so discouraged and lonely!

As silly as it seems, let me find at least a brief respite in romantic books and movies. Though I am living vicariously, let these times keep the dream of romance alive for me. I know it will happen someday for me. I must be patient and wait for the real thing to come along.

Bitterness

Help me not to be bitter, Lord! There is so much I *could* be bitter about, so much unfairness in my life.

Let me not choose the path of *bitterness* but of *betterness*. (Yes, God! I made up a new word!)

Let me take the high road, the better path. Let me concentrate not on all that I've lost but on all that I've gained.

My life is truer, richer, and more spiritual than ever before. I see small gifts now as wonderful and treasured ones.

Though it is sometimes hard to see, let me realize my life is better now.

Waiting

It seems like I'm always waiting for something, God—for the doctor or the dentist, in traffic, in line at the store, for the right man to come into my life. I feel like most of my life is spent waiting!

Whenever I am waiting for something, let me fill my moments with whatever richness I can. If I'm at a doctor or dentist's appointment, I can read or chat with another person. At a store I can do the same. In traffic I can listen to quiet music and reflect on my life. And while I am waiting for that special man to come into my life, I can concentrate on making myself the best *me* I can possibly be!

Happy Birthday

I'd like to just skip my birthday, God. The kids don't really bother with it or remember, and there's no special someone to plan a romantic dinner.

Though I may not celebrate this day with cake and presents, let me quietly celebrate the gift of me.

Let me celebrate the woman I have become— a warm, wise, wonderful woman, compassionate and kind, a good mother and a loving friend.

Let me be grateful for all the gifts you have given me and those yet to come.

Happy Birthday, Dear Heart!

My Journal

I'm not saying I'm a great writer, God. But it certainly is good therapy for me to write in a journal each day.

I write each morning before the kids are up. I sit with my cup of tea and write whatever comes into my head.

I buy myself pretty journals—all on sale, of course. It doesn't matter what I write, just that I take this time for myself each day.

I meet myself on these pages, and I can write whatever I please. There are no critics here. These pages are just for me!

I've come to think of my journal as a silent, unbiased friend. No one judges or silences my words or thoughts. It is my safe haven.

(Hmmm....Maybe this is better than therapy!)

Food

Nope. This isn't another diet prayer, God. Today I pray for more spiritual nourishment, a replenishment of my soul.

I am trying to feed my spirit with prayer and reflection, but there's not always time in this life of mine.

I guess I need something like fast food for my soul.

Is it possible for you to serve me up some quick graces, a heaping plate of patience and a sprinkling of serenity?

I sure could use a good, quick meal just now.

And today I can plan to make more time for spiritual nourishment.

Self-love

I'd be lying if I said I didn't want to meet a wonderful man, God. But it's not as important to me as it once was. (OK, God, so I used to be downright desperate to meet someone!)

I'm so much more comfortable with myself now. It's taken me a great while to get to this place. But I like the woman I am still becoming. She is strong, courageous, and beautiful of spirit. (I am growing fonder of her every day!)

I won't say my self-esteem is as good as it should be. But I'm liking myself a little more each day.

(And the more I'm liking me, the more likable I'll be when the man of my dreams does show up!)

Morning Cup

A cup of tea might not sound like much, God, but it is another one of those small blessings in my life.

Each morning I find some quiet time just for me—before the kids are up. I sit with my cup of tea (a fresh wedge of lemon makes me feel like I'm at a four-star restaurant). I snuggle in my favorite chair and write in my journal, do a daily reading, and reflect a bit on my life.

This is *my* time. I spend most of my day working and caring for others. But this small joy—a morning cup and time for me—is mine alone.

I am grateful for it!

About My
Children

School Events

It's time to do it again, Lord—go to another event alone. It may be Open House Night for my son, where I find a seat and listen to the animated conversations of the couples all around me. It might be my child's soccer game that I dutifully attend each weekend, cheering my daughter on as I watch the smiling couples sipping coffee together. It might even be opening night for the school play. I dress my best and get there early to sit in the front row. I fumble with the new video camera as I record my daughter's precious moments.

Please bless each of these events for me. They are concrete symbols of the deep love I have for my child. Though they are sometimes painful and lonely for me, let me realize that all this is for them! Let me attend each event with joy and great pride in my child's talents and achievements.

Let me not fear these events but welcome them as a sure sign of my love for my child, and help me realize that all these events are memories in the making!

Mealtimes

I pray for our mealtimes, Lord, because we don't share them often. Breakfast is a solitary, hurried affair. No one is home for lunch. And family dinners are a struggle to put together.

I tried making family dinners a ritual and tradition, but it didn't work out as I'd planned. It seems much harder to pull this off when there's only one parent.

Let me not concentrate on the quantity of family meals but on the quality of the ones we share together.

Even if we sit together for five minutes, let those minutes be precious and loving.

Let me realize that a hamburger in a fast-food restaurant can feel like the finest feast—if you enjoy it as a family!

Keep My Children Safe

Please keep my children safe, Lord. As they get older and are more and more out of my sight, protect them with your loving arms.

The saying goes that "God couldn't be everywhere, so God created mothers." While my children are not with me, I know that you will protect them, for they are your children, too!

Thank you, Lord, for keeping my children safe.

Eating Out

We don't eat out very often, Lord. When we do it's not the fancier places we used to go.

But I am so grateful for any food someone else prepares—even if it's pizza or burgers.

Candlelight and fancy china has nothing over checkered tablecloths and paper plates when I am sharing a meal with my children.

Let us appreciate this special blessing. I welcome it as a little break from the kitchen and a time to share more relaxed conversation with my children.

Going to the Movies

I'll bet there's never been a prayer about going to the movies, God. But it has become a special family treat for us.

It is a time when there needs to be no conversation and hence, no disagreements—as long as we can agree on the movie choice! It is a time of pure entertainment, relaxation, and escape…and boy, with all the stress in our hectic lives, a little respite is most welcome.

Thank you for this little break. It is much appreciated. (And the buttered popcorn's not bad either!)

Mom's Taxi

Please bless this driver and vehicle, Lord. I get so tired sometimes of chauffeuring my kids back and forth to all of their activities. I wish I could call in sick and have someone fill in for me. But I can't.

Help me to realize that it's only a short time in my life that I'll be doing this. There will come a time when my children will be driving on their own. (I may even miss their choice of music then—well, maybe not.)

Bless this vehicle and all of those inside it. Keep us all safe in your loving arms.

Memories

I pray for two kinds of memories today, God—the old ones we made and the new ones we're making now.

Please bless the old memories. Though some are still painful to remember, let me select the happier ones instead. Let me put these in a bright, cheerful scrapbook in my mind.

Bless the new memories, too. Let me realize that our new little family is making its own fresh memories. These, too, I will place in my mental scrapbook.

So bless *all* of our memories, God—the old ones past and the new ones in the making!

Traditions

It seems like so many old traditions are gone now. The holidays just aren't the same. They are lonelier now. They are different. I'm afraid of all these changes, God!

Help me to create new traditions for my children and me. It might be fun to rattle things up a bit! Maybe Easter could be a fancy brunch out and a trip to the movies. Maybe Christmas Eve could be a pizza picnic in front of the tree.

Let me find creative new traditions that my children will remember with a smile of love!

College

I pray today, Lord, for the resources to send my children to college. Right now so much energy is taken up providing for our day-to-day existence. College seems a distant thing to worry about.

But help me to find small ways to prepare for it, both financially and emotionally. Guide me to creative solutions so that my children can go to college. And help me deal with the idea of living on my own without them some day. We are such a close little unit. (Well, on our good days, that is!) I will miss even the nagging voices and messy rooms.

Let me see college not as a *loss* of my children but a *gaining* of their own wings.

Help me to provide this opportunity for my children to *soar*!

Vacation

Thank you for this vacation, Lord. Though we may not be flying off to Tahiti, it is wonderful just to have some time off. We need some time together as a family, and I need this time to renew myself.

Let us find comfort in being alone together, and help us to appreciate each other more. Let us keep the outside world away for just a little while. Let us relax and refresh ourselves so we can go back to the world with more energy.

Prayer for My Children

This may be my longest prayer, Lord, because it is my children I worry about most in all of this.

Am I giving them all they need? I feel guilty that they don't have the two-parent family that many of their friends do.

Help me to realize that as long as I am doing my best, I am giving them what they need.

I pray that my children are healthy—not only physically but emotionally, mentally, and spiritually as well.

Let them find work that stimulates and energizes their minds. Let them find spiritual food to nourish their souls. And let them not be jaded by this divorce. Let them still believe in the gift and grace of love. When it is their time, let them find a love that enhances their lives and completes them as human beings.

I pray that my children lead joyous, fulfilling lives. I pray that I can help them achieve this and that I can help give them wings to soar when it is their time to discover the sky!

Shopping With My Daughter

Lord, I think I need more stamina for shopping with my daughter than I do for working a twelve-hour day!

I need more patience than I do for waiting in a two-hour line!

Let me see these not as unpleasant tasks but as opportunities for my daughter and I to be together.

Let me smile when I hear the knowing laughter of others in the fitting room as they listen to our exchange.

As I wait patiently to see the next outfit, let me remember how blessed I am to have a daughter. (Maybe next time I'll even remember to bring a book to read as I wait!)

Spiritual Health for My Children

I pray today, God, for the spiritual health of my children. They don't like going to church. They say, "It's boring." Though I try to stress how much they can get out of it, they don't listen to me!

Please help me to believe that they *are* learning by my example. Though their faith may be hard for me to see, it is there—deep within their souls. I have planted the seed. I must wait patiently for the flower.

About My
Challenges

Grocery Shopping

I used to hate grocery shopping, Lord. It was just one more chore to do.

But now that I am the sole provider for my family, it has taken on a new meaning.

I feel a deep sense of gratitude and abundance as I shop for my family and then unpack the food in my tiny kitchen. I am more grateful than I ever was for the simple gift of food and for being able to provide for my children.

I almost feel like an ancient hunter who returns with the family's next meal! It is a feeling of great pride for me and deep gratitude. A mundane task has taken on new meaning!

Sole Provider

It is scary to be the sole provider for my family, God. I'm not used to it, but I'm becoming used to it quickly.

Sometimes—oftentimes perhaps—I waste my energy being envious of the married couples who enjoy rich lifestyles. I see that the man has a great income, and maybe the wife works, too, but doesn't really have to.

Let me not squander my needed energy on such thoughts. Let me instead focus on creative ways to increase my income to provide for my family or to find clever ways to save or stretch money as well.

Let me feel great pride in knowing that all the hours I work directly benefit my children. This infuses me with great energy—knowing it is done FOR my children!

Diet Prayer

Please help me to lose weight, Lord. I'm having so much trouble! I want to look and feel healthier. I know what I *should* do, but I can't seem to find the strength to do it.

I get started and lose my willpower. Something stressful comes up and I blow it.

Please be with me during this struggle. Help me to really and truly make a commitment to myself. Let me be as committed to *myself* as I am to my *children*!

Let me realize that by doing something for my *own* health, I'm not only giving a gift to myself, but to my children as well.

Mistakes

Please bless my mistakes, Lord, for I've made so many of them. (If you turn them all into blessings, I'll be a very rich woman indeed!)

Let me realize that my mistakes have brought me to the place where I am today, and I am at a much better place than I was several years ago! My mistakes were really fruitful lessons that made my life richer in a myriad of ways.

Maybe my mistakes really are blessings after all, and maybe I already *am* a rich woman!

Forgiveness

God, I find this prayer a difficult one because I'm not sure I can do it yet.

But help me to simply *think* about forgiving my ex-husband for all he has done—the pain he has caused us.

Let me remember that along with this pain, he gave me the most incredible gift of my life—my children. Perhaps I can try to forgive him because of them.

Even if I'm not ready to forgive today, I can at least *think* about it. For in *forgiving* him I am actually *giving* a great gift to myself as well—the gift of freedom!

Mountains of Laundry

No one would believe I really have a mountain of laundry, Lord, but I do! I keep washing and drying clothes, and then my children come in and toss clean clothes on the floor with dirty ones. So I keep washing the same clothes over and over!

I know it seems ridiculous, but there are so many tasks for me to do and not enough time to do them all. Help me realize that with laundry, as in life, I must break each big task into smaller chunks. I should just do the best I can and then let it go. If I work on something a little at a time, I can accomplish anything— even making a mountain of laundry disappear!

Bless This Mess

Today, God, I ask you to bless this mess. I can't seem to keep up with all the housework. I feel ashamed when I look at my messy house. I feel I should be able to do it all.

Help me realize that I really *can't* do it all! There are some things I'll need to let go. Having the neatest house is one of them.

I need to prioritize things in my life more since I am alone. My first priority is providing for my children—and that means my job comes before the state of my home.

Let me know that a tidier house than mine doesn't mean it's a more *loving* home. There may be a lot of clutter in my house, but there's a lot of something else, too—love. And I'm grateful that my home is brimful of that!

Bills

Wow! They're *all mine* now, Lord. Every bill I get has my name on it. It feels scary to me sometimes to realize I have all this responsibility.

Please help me settle quietly as I pay my bills. Bless me as I attend to each one. Help me to realize that all of this is for my family's welfare.

Let me not begrudge this task but realize how lucky I am to have the money to pay my bills. And if money gets tight, let me find a creative way to deal with it.

Please bless me as I pay my bills and bless all this paperwork.

(And if you'd like to use a little divine intervention, I'd welcome a refund check, too!)

The Future

The future scares me, God. It is this looming unknown thing that might swallow me up with "What ifs?"

Let me not concentrate on my *fears* for the future, but my hopes and dreams instead.

Let me see the future as a lovely banquet of sweet possibilities. I am the honored guest, free to sample all the delicacies!

Who knows what delights the future might bring? Let me look at the future not with *fear* but a smile of joy!

Escape

I may not have the means or money to get away right now, God, but I long for an *escape* from my life right now.

This lonely road is tough. (I don't see any palm trees on it!)

Please help me to find ways to make little detours, to escape for just a little while. Whether with a book, a bath, or a cup of tea, I need to cultivate quiet moments where I can renew myself and return to my life rejuvenated and refreshed.

Envy

I know envy is a sin, Lord, but I wouldn't be honest if I denied feeling it.

It is so easy to feel envious of others—their houses, their cars, their apparently happy, together families.

Let me not feel envy in my heart for what I *don't* have but joy in my heart for all I *do* have.

And, Lord, you have blessed me with so much! May I be grateful for the abundance in my life, and may I celebrate the richness of it all.

Money

A prayer about money may seem strange, God, but it has become a big concern as I travel this road.

Help me to find peace about this. Let me not become obsessed with how much money I have or lack. But make me wiser in how I deal with it.

Let me try to remember that I am not part of a two-income family anymore. There is just one income now—mine. Our lives have changed accordingly.

Let me concentrate on being grateful for the money I *do* have and my ability to support our family.

Discipline

Somehow discipline flies out the window, Lord, once someone becomes a single mother. (At least it has for me!)

There is simply not enough strength inside of me anymore to be *consistent* all the time. Our lives have become *inconsistent*. Everything seems to be in a constant state of flux. Things not only change on a monthly, weekly, or daily basis but somehow by the hour, even minute.

I choose my battles accordingly. Let me realize that though I may have a *lack* of discipline in my home, there is an *abundance* of love!

Feeling Safe

I don't often feel safe these days, God. I long to feel safe again.

I feel afraid of so many things. It feels like anyone or anything could bring me to tears.

Please infuse me with strength. Let me not search for big, strong arms to help me. Let me wrap my arms around myself instead. Let me be my own strength—with your help.

Let this strength slowly build and grow into the warmth and comfort of feeling safe.

Dating

Dating scares me, Lord. I was part of a couple for so long. To even *think* about trying to meet someone new makes me want to run to a convent!

Let me approach dating with a smile of hope. Let me leave my comfort zone and seek the friendship of a man. (As the saying goes, "You don't have to *marry* the man.") Let me find the friendship of a man first.

There are nice men out there who seek companionship as much as I do. Let me be open to the idea of dating and the wonderful opportunities it presents.

Father's Day

Just as I celebrate Mother's Day, I will celebrate this day, too, Lord—for I am both mother *and* father to my children.

Today I thank you, too, as our heavenly Father. Thank you for keeping my family under your constant care and for all the blessings you've given us.

Please bless the father of my children. Though I find it difficult to bless the man that has caused such pain, help me to do it for my children. Please help him to put his own children first and to realize that even though I am no longer his wife, they will *always* be his children!

Miss Fix-It

There's no one here to fix things, Lord, except me.

Whether it's a blown fuse or a broken dishwasher flooding my kitchen, I must deal with it. I may not *want* to deal with all of this on top of everything else, but I must.

Give me the can-do attitude I need. Help me to try a task, and if it's not something I can accomplish, guide me to the person who can. Help me find repair people who are honest and reasonable. Let me see these new tasks not as *problems* but as *opportunities* to increase my self-confidence.

Stress Magnet

I feel like a stress magnet, Lord. Do I attract all these worries and stress to myself somehow? I'm beginning to wonder.

I know that being a single mom automatically means more stress and responsibility. But I know other single mothers who seem to have it more together than I do.

Please help me to see that this too shall pass. My life may seem too full to handle right now. But I am doing my best, and I *am* handling it. It may not be easy, and I may not be perfect, but life will not always be this stressful.

As I look forward to a more peaceful future, let me find small ways to attract serenity in my life *now*.

Magic Mirror

Today I pray for a magic mirror, God. I'd like one into which I look and see a thinner, prettier me. I'd like to see fewer wrinkles and a more youthful face, a face full of energy.

Let me look beyond my mirror today. Let me look deep inside the woman I have become. There is a beauty that radiates within, a beauty that comes from all I have learned on this difficult journey. This beauty doesn't come from a fountain of youth but from a vast sea of wisdom. I have learned so much—about life and about myself.

Let me look in the mirror and see what others already see—a vibrant woman, a survivor whose beauty shines through in her dancing eyes and inviting smile.

Hmm…maybe my mirror *can* be magic after all.

Survivor

Today I give thanks that I am a survivor, Lord! It is mostly because of my faith in you that I have endured.

There have been so many times I've wanted to simply throw in the proverbial towel, to give up. But you wouldn't let me. You've stood by my children and me, your invisible arms guiding me, your silent voice encouraging me not to give up.

Thank you for the deep inner strength it takes to be a survivor and for the faith that always keeps me strong.

Direction

I could use some signposts today, God, to point me in the right direction.

There are so many decisions to make, and now I have to make them all myself. What if I make the wrong choices? It doesn't affect just me but my children as well.

Though I may not see a glaring sign directing me, let me look deep within for answers. Let me listen to my gut, my intuition—for then I know I will be heading in the right direction!

Letting Go

I pray today, God, for the ability to let go of more things in my life.

So much is *not* within my control, for instance, what other people do or say. I especially want the father of my children to be a warm and wonderful dad. But if he's not, let me realize that I have no control over it whatsoever.

Show me how to put my energy into all the things I have control over and to do those things fully.

Help me let go of all those things and people in my life that I cannot control. Let all this slip as easily as water through my mind. Let me hold on instead to the serenity that comes from letting go.

Table for One

OK, Lord, I'm finally going to do it—go out to eat by myself. I am going to push past my fear of being gawked at and eat a meal out.

When the host or hostess asks "How many?" I will not shrink and mutter, "Oh. Just me." (Gulp.) I will smile graciously and say, "One please!"

When I am seated, please give me the confidence to be comfortable by myself, to eat slowly and enjoy my meal.

Let this be one more successful venture outside my comfort zone. Let me smile at the families and couples I see and perhaps even wink at the others dining alone.

Let me be proud of one more positive step on this path.

(And let me give myself a break if I *do* pull that paperback out of my purse!)

My Children's Father

Though our life together as a couple has ended, our new lives are still connected through our children. It is often difficult and uncomfortable.

Help me to do my best, Lord, when dealing with my children's father. Let me keep an inner garden of calm, though outside it is stormy. I will try to comfort myself by knowing I do everything for the highest good.

Let my faith in you be the fence that protects my garden, as well as the sun that nourishes it. Though storms may threaten, my faith holds fast and sustains me.

Fear of Commitment

I am afraid of getting close to someone again and being hurt. I don't think I could live through this again, Lord.

Let me face my future with a smile of hope in my soul. Let me realize that without risk, I will gain nothing.

If I am to love again, I need to take chances. I need to trust again.

I cannot be certain things will work out. But I am certain of one thing: you put us on this earth to love and be loved. This is not accomplished without risk. If I am to find the one who will love me long and well, I must take chances. I must follow my heart and let go.

Be with me, Lord, as I walk this new path. If I falter, I know you are always there to pick me up again. Let me walk toward my dream, away from the darkness and on toward the light.

About My World

Pets

Today I give thanks for our pets, Lord. Whether they have been with us a long time or are new additions to our family, they are an integral part of our lives.

They bring us comfort and love. They are symbols of enduring love—unconditional love.

I give thanks for our pets and ask a special blessing for their continued health.

Winter

Oh, Lord, I need a prayer about winter! I've never liked this cold, dreary season where everything is dead outside. It feels like hope dies in winter.

Help me to kindle the flame of hope and dreams of spring during this longest season.

Let me find small joys that only winter can bring—the sparkle of freshly fallen snow, a fragrant cup of hot chocolate, the warmth of a roaring fire, the comfort of a single candle flame, or curling up in flannel to read a good book.

I will take this time to settle inside my comfortable home and perhaps to settle inside myself, too. To spend time in thought and perhaps dreaming of the inevitable spring!

Church

When I was first alone, it was so difficult going to church. As I sat there with my children, I felt like we were lepers somehow. We were missing a piece of our family—the father.

I would stare longingly at the happy families gathered there and feel the tears begin. It was so painful, Lord!

Time has eased that pain. Now when I go to church, I focus less on the people around me and more on the real reason I'm there—to fortify and feed my own spirit!

I am nourished by the words I hear. I am strengthened to go back to my life and face what I must.

At first I looked more at the *outside* of what went on in church, but now I focus more on the *inside*.

Home

This is a tough prayer, God. I want to be grateful for the home we have, but it is so much smaller than our last one and not as nice. I feel envious of those with bigger, nicer houses. I regret the loss of our family home.

Let me concentrate on the word *home* and not *house*. House is simply a space, big or small, where people live. Home is so much more—a comfortable, welcoming place where a family lives and loves together.

My home may be small, but it is warm and welcoming. We live here as a family. Despite its size, this home is filled to brimming with love. Let me be grateful for that!

Spring

It's spring again, God, and I am so happy! It has been a long, lonely winter, cold and dreary. I am so grateful for the sunshine that greens the earth and seeps inside of me, spreading its warmth and hope.

I feel renewed seeing all the blossoming flowers. I realize that spring always *does* follow winter, and so will it be with my own life.

My dark times are slowly brightening. I can finally begin to see the sun melting the darkness.

I see spring all around me—but more important, I *feel* it in my soul!

Girlfriends

I wouldn't mind a male friend right now, God, but it is my girlfriends I pray for today.

I give thanks for their love and guidance, their sunny words throughout my darkest days. I don't know how I could ever do this completely on my own.

I suppose these friends are really angels you've sent down to help ease my way.

I thank you for the gift of girlfriends and ask a special blessing just for them—that they may know sweet joy all the days of their lives!

Understanding

I pray for understanding, God, especially that of my family. They seem to treat me as if everything's still the same. It's not. Our world has changed forever.

My parents think I can still be a perfect mother and discipline my children accordingly.

Nothing is the same, God! I simply don't have the energy and resources I used to have.

Please help those who love me understand that I am doing the very best I can under the circumstances. Help them to love and accept me as I am right now, this very day.

I could use their prayers and understanding as my companions on this walk. I pray for this today.

Compassion

Now that I am a single mother, Lord, I seem to have a lot more compassion in my heart. Since I have been through so much with my children, I am especially understanding of others who are going through the same thing.

I would pray today, however, for the compassion of others *not* going through this...for those of us living through it.

How can they understand something they've never been through?

Help them try not to judge me so quickly but to realize we all live different lives. What is right for them may not work in my circumstances. Let them try to be open, understanding, and compassionate.

And if they find it difficult to understand why I do things, let them at least *accept* it with compassion.

My Job

I pray for my job today, Lord. It is crucial to the daily existence of my family.

Things at work don't always go easily. Sometimes I feel like quitting.

Let me concentrate on the positive at work, on all the things I do so well. Let me work mindfully, concentrating on whatever task is before me. Let me face each day at work as a new day, a fresh start. And let me be grateful for the job that enables me to provide food, clothing, shelter, and comforts for my children and me.

Shopping

Keep me out of the fancy stores, Lord. I don't know why I look in them at all. (Perhaps it has something to do with having a teenage daughter.)

The glossy displays beckon to me even as the rich clients seem to silently ask, "What business do *you* have here?"

I feel frustrated not being able to give my children and myself all the material things we want. But the reality is that I can't.

Let me concentrate instead on all we *can* and already do have. There is an abundance of love in our home. (I'd rather have that than designer sheets any day!)

If I do go into fancy stores, let me walk with pride and certainty. I deserve to be there as much as anyone else. Let me enjoy the visual feast before my eyes. Perhaps I'll even be inspired to find creative ways to duplicate some of the ideas I see.

Let me realize that anyone can spend money, but not everyone can use what they already have in creative ways, making less into more!

Parties

I'm so tired of going to parties and family gatherings, Lord. I smile and act sociable, but inside I'm crying because I'm so lonely.

The world seems set up for couples—tables for two, a double room, and invitations to "Mr. and Mrs." all make me feel left out.

Let me try to forget that I'm not part of a couple. I am, however, a vibrant person on my own. I wouldn't be invited to a party or gathering unless people really wanted me there. Let me enjoy these festive times, savoring these special people in my life. I am a complete person on my own. Let me celebrate the person I have become!

My Second Job

I seem to pray a lot of prayers for *strength*, Lord. I need it for this one, too!

Give me the stamina I need for my second job—the one that begins when I walk in my door each night.

I know married women work, too, but at least there's someone else to share this second job.

Help me to simply do the best I can. I can ask my children to help, and I can accept the job they do, even if it's not perfect.

I can learn to slack off a little where my second job is concerned. After all, I'm my *own* boss here!

Holidays

I used to feel such joy and anticipation at this time of year. Now I find such loneliness.

Please fill me with the glowing spirit of hope. Let me bask in the love of my family and friends. Let me find the quiet joys in each day of this season. Let me treasure the gifts you have for me, if I only will open them—sweet joy, peace, faith, hope, and love. These gifts are mine to unwrap and treasure each day of my life.

Christmas Spirit

I can't believe it, God! I've finally got the Christmas spirit back! It's taken such a long time. But I've finally begun to feel a new birth of joy inside myself—an abundance of hope!

My family, my friends, but mostly my kids can't believe it. Christmas was always my favorite holiday, and yet I've abandoned my seasonal joy for years now.

Well—it's back! I am throwing myself into the holiday like a woman who's been starving for a meal and now has a bounty before her.

My spirit is joyful and abundant now. People are catching my holiday spirit like an affectionate bug!

I am planting warmth and smiles wherever I go.

At this special time of your birth, I am finally reborn, too!

Epilogue: S.M.U.F.F.

I know you've never heard this word, God. But this is a prayer for an organization, a support group that only exists in my mind.

It is a group that I think would be a wonderful, healing place for single moms like me. It wouldn't be for deep conversations or confessions (though I'm sure there'd be plenty of each). The main idea would be to give single moms the one thing I know is sorely lacking in my own life—fun!

"Single Moms Unite For Fun!"

I pray that one day there is a group of single moms that meet to simply have fun—to see a movie or discuss books or do a craft or go for a walk. Anything to do as long as it's fun!

There's so much work and stress in our lives. What we lack most is fun.

Single moms everywhere, form your own little S.M.U.F.F. groups—even if it's with just one other single mom.

Remember what incredible moms and women you are! You deserve some fun in your life and highest regards for one of the most difficult jobs of all—not just being a mom but doing it on your own!

I hereby make you an honorary member of S.M.U.F.F. Spread the word of joy to all the other single moms you know!